Water

Water

Diane McClymont

 GARRETT EDUCATIONAL CORPORATION

Edited by Richard Young

Text © 1991 by Garrett Educational Corporation First
Published in the United States in 1991 by Garrett
Educational Corporation, 130 East 13th Street, Ada,
Oklahoma 74820

First Published in 1987 by Macdonald & Co. (Publishers)
Ltd., London with the title WATER © 1987 Macdonald &
Co. (Publishers) Ltd.

Manufactured in the United States of America.

Library of Congress Cataloging - in - Publication Data
McClymont, Diane.
      Water / McClymont, Diane.
          p. cm. — (First technology library)
      Summary: Discusses the properties, uses, and
      problems of water and suggests water-related
      projects.
      ISBN 1-56074-006-X
      1. Water-supply — Juvenile literature. 2.
      Water-power — Juvenile literature. 3. Water —
      Juvenile literature. [1. Water.]
      I. Title   II. Series
      TD348.M33   1991
      553.7 — dc20   91-20536
                                              CIP
                                              AC

How to use this book

First, look at the Contents page opposite.
Read the list to see if it includes the
subject you want. The list tells you what
each page is about, so you can find the
page with the information you need.

In this book. some words are **darker** than
others. These are harder words.
Sometimes there is a picture to explain
the word. For example, the words **water
cycle** appear on page 8, and there is a
picture of it on pages 8 and 9. Other
words are explained in the Word List on
page 31.

On page 28 you will find a technology
project. This project suggests ideas and
starting points for learning more about
technology by yourself.

CONTENTS

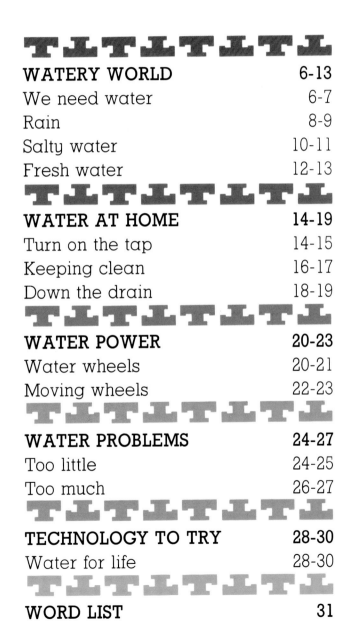

We need water

We drink it, bath in it, splash in it. We sail on it, wash clothes in it, cook food with it. It can heat things up or cool things down. It can be freezing ice or scalding steam. Sometimes it is invisible. What is this wonderful thing? It is ... water.

Without water, we would die. More than half of the human body is water. People, animals, birds, fish, insects, plants and trees need water to live.

We live in a watery world. If you were an astronaut looking down on our world, you would think Earth a funny name for our planet. A better name would be Planet Water, as nearly three-quarters of the world's surface is covered by water. The oceans and seas are salt water. The water on land, such as in streams and rivers, ponds and lakes, is not salty. It is called **fresh** water. It comes from the rain. We need this water to survive. You could go for weeks without food, but without water you would die in a few days. Just to stay alive, you need one or two quarts of water each day.

Without water, everything in our world would die.

Rain

When it rains
they put their heads down and walk
faster.
But I want to stand still
look up
and see the drops
falling.

Kathy Henderson

Where does our rain come from? It all begins with the sun shining on the seas, rivers, puddles or your wet clothes drying on the clothes line. As the water becomes warm, tiny bits of it, too small to see, rise into the air as **water vapor.** This drying is called evaporation.

As the water vapor rises higher into the air, it cools. It changes back into minute drops of water, forming clouds. This cooling back into water is called condensation. The clouds float along and as they climb higher, they become colder. Small drop of water become bigger drops. Eventually, the drops are too heavy to stay in the sky and fall to the ground as rain. The rain runs into streams and rivers. They flow into the sea and the whole process begins again. This is called the **water cycle**.

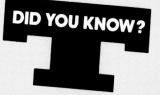

DID YOU KNOW?

How much rain?

Some places in the world, such as in India, Hawaii and Africa, have almost 400 inches of rain a year.

In other parts of the world, such as in Chile, it hasn't rained for over 400 years.

If the raindrops pass through very cold air as they fall to earth, they freeze and fall as hail. When the weather is very cold, the tiny drops of water in the clouds freeze. They become ice crystals that grow bigger and fall as snowflakes.

Salty water

"Water, water everywhere, nor any drop to drink." These words come from a poem called "The Ancient Mariner" by S.T. Coleridge. In this poem, a sailor will die of thirst because he cannot drink the salty seawater.

The salt in the oceans is the kind we put on our food. It is found in rocks. As rivers flow along, they **dissolve** the salt in the rocks and carry it out to sea. When seawater **evaporates**, the salt is left behind and the sea becomes salty.

Why do waves happen?

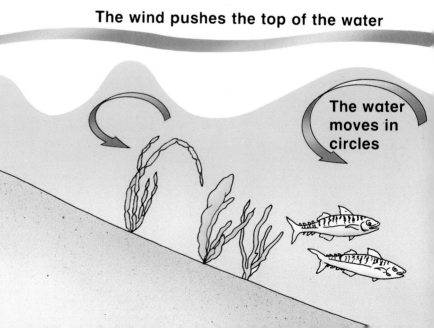

The wind pushes the top of the water

The waves crash on to the shore

The water moves in circles

The sea moves up and down as the wave passes through it

Some machines make electricity from the waves

Where the sea meets the land is the shoreline. Most shores have a **tide**. Twice a day the sea moves in and out over the shore. At high tide the beach can be covered and waves crash onto it. At low tide the beach is uncovered. The tides are caused by a pulling effect on the seas from the sun and moon. Waves are made by the wind, the tides and the shape of the land. The stronger the wind, the bigger the waves. The waves travel across the surface of the sea. The water doesn't move along. It just goes up and down as the waves pass through it. Near the land the waves grow taller. The top of the wave moves faster than the bottom, curls over and crashes down. Both the tides and the waves can be used to make electricity.

11

Fresh water

The water in streams and rivers, ponds and lakes is not salty. It is **fresh** water.

When it rains, some of the water soaks into the ground. People used to dig down until they found this underground water. Then they built a well. Later, pumps were used to draw up the water.

In some places water bubbles up out of the ground as a spring. Springs and streams join together to make rivers. We get most of our water from rivers.

As towns and cities grew, more and more water was needed. Now we collect the rainwater from rivers in huge lakes that we call **reservoirs**.

Sometimes water **engineers** build reservoirs in the mountains where few people live. They find a deep valley with a river flowing through it. First the bed of the river is tested to find firm rock. Then a dam is built to block up the end of the valley and stop the river from flowing.

The dam must be very strong. The walls are made of thick **concrete** built into the sides of the mountain. The dam holds back the river so that the water floods the valley. Other kinds of reservoirs are made on flat land by digging a hole and building up banks around it. This kind of reservoir looks like a long hill until you get to the top of the bank and see the water inside.

A reservoir holds millions of gallons of water. It is stored there until it is needed.

Getting water from a well in a bucket is hard work

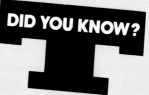

Turn on the faucet

When you turn on the faucet at home, clean water comes gushing out. The water in a **reservoir** can be dirty and has to be cleaned at the waterworks. It is pumped to sand and gravel **filter beds**. As the water soaks through the beds, the dirt is left behind.

The water is then pumped through machines that add **chlorine** to kill any harmful germs that are left.

The clean water is then pumped through big underground pipes called **mains**. Smaller pipes lead off the big pipes to take water to every house.

Where the water pipe enters the house, there is a device called the **stopcock** to turn the water on and off.

In some parts of the world, the cold water pipe takes water to the cold faucet in the kitchen and to a water storage tank in the attic. The water level in this tank is controlled by a **ball valve**. A hollow ball on a rod floats up with the water, and a valve stops the flow of water at the right level. Pipes from this storage tank take cold water to the cold faucets in the bathroom and to a water tank for heating water. Other pipes then take the hot water to all the hot faucets in the house. As the hot water is used, more cold water flows into the heater.

____ Cold water

____ Hot water

____ Waste

How does a faucet work?

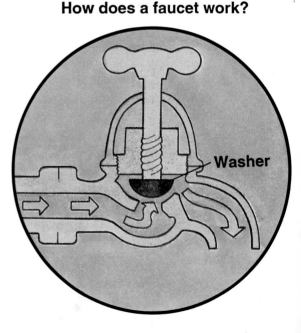

Washer

Cold water storage tank

Ball valve

How much do you use?
Our great, great grandparents used about 18 quarts of water a day. Some people use about 120 quarts each day. Others use more; others, far less.

Can you estimate how much water you use in a day?

Stopcock

Mains

15

Keeping clean

Years ago people carried their washing to a stream and rubbed it with stones and water to loosen the dirt. The wet clothes were dried in the sun. In some countries washing is still done this way.

Then along came some great **inventions**! A washboard was a grooved board to rub clothes on. A dolly was like a three-legged stool with a long handle. It was swirled around in a tub to get the dirt out. Washing was hard work. Machines now make it easy.

The first washing machine was worked by hand. It was a tub with a dolly fitted in the lid that was turned by a handle. Then electric motors were attached.

Washing machines can now heat the water, wash, spin dry and tumble dry **automatically**. The washing time and temperature can be changed to wash different kinds of fabrics.

When the washer is turned on, hot and cold water go into a drum through pipes at the back of the machine. The water mixes with soap powder and the clothes spin around in hot, soapy water to get out the dirt. The drum, run by an electric motor, spins at great speed. All the water is carried away to a drain through a pipe at the bottom.

Doing the washing about 100 years ago

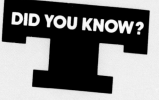
How much water?
A modern automatic washing machine uses 35 to 45 gallons of water for each load of washing.

Modern washing machine

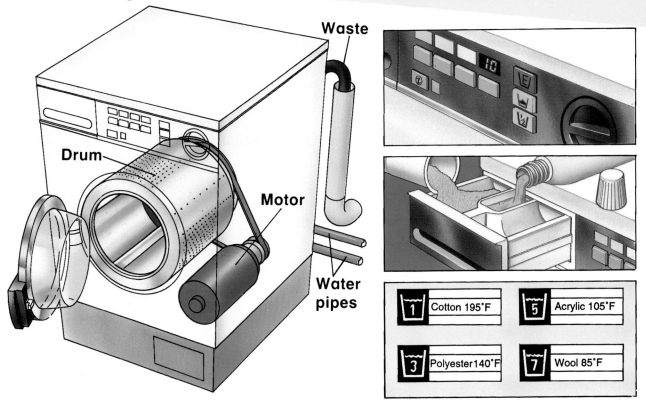

Waste

Drum

Motor

Water pipes

1	Cotton 195°F		5	Acrylic 105°F
3	Polyester 140°F		7	Wool 85°F

Down the drain

Have you ever watched the dirty water gurgling down the drain?

All the dirty water from our homes, schools, factories and streets goes down the drain into large underground pipes called **sewers**. Years ago, people used to throw all their rubbish and dirty water into a kind of gutter in the street called an open sewer. The germs often made people ill.

Today, our dirty water, called sewage, goes through the sewer to be cleaned at the sewage works.

When the sewage arrives at the works, it passes through a big tank where large particles, called grit, are removed. Then it moves on to a **settling tank**, where small particles sink to the bottom of the tank to form a **sludge**. This sludge is treated with special organisms, called bacteria, that eat, or **digest**, all the harmful waste. The treated sludge is used by farmers to **fertilize** the soil.

The liquid sewage moves on into an **aeration tank** or **filter bed**. Air is bubbled through the tanks as more bacteria digest the waste. Finally, the almost clean water passes through fine pebbles where any remaining particles are removed.

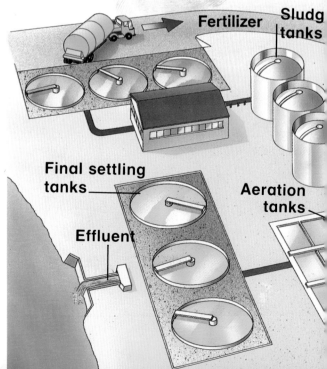

Fertilizer

Sludge tanks

Final settling tanks

Aeration tanks

Effluent

The treated water is called **effluent** and is returned to the river. If we put dirty water into the river, it would kill plants, fish and other animals. This is called **pollution**.

Modern sewage works

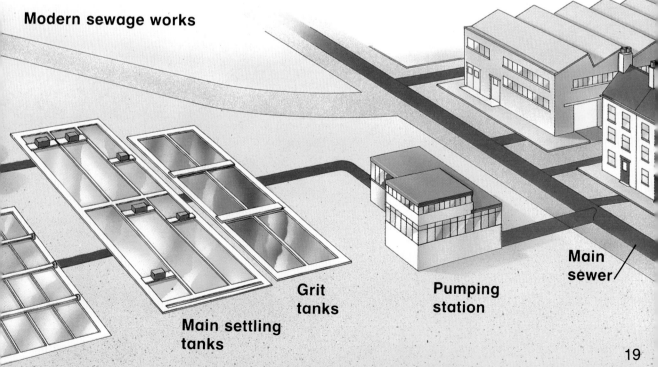

Main settling tanks

Grit tanks

Pumping station

Main sewer

Water wheels

A flowing river is strong. Its power can turn wheels. Long ago, waterwheels were used to run all kinds of machines. A flour mill might have a waterwheel outside. This turned the **millstones** inside, grinding corn into flour.

There are two kinds of waterwheels: an **undershot** wheel and an **overshot** wheel. Can you find out how they got their names?

Today, rivers are used to turn wheels to make electricity.

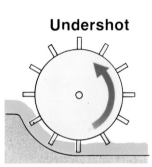

Undershot

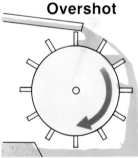

Overshot

Reservoir

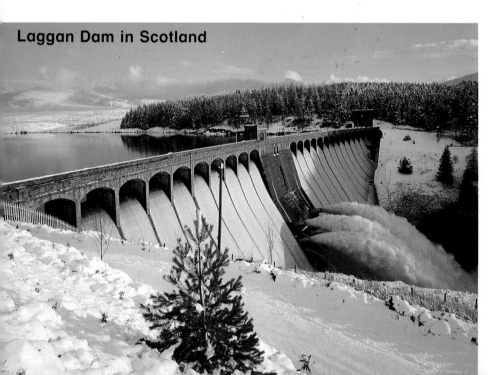

Laggan Dam in Scotland

Electricity that is made by using water is called hydroelectricity. "Hydro" is a Greek word meaning "water."

Hydroelectric power stations are usually built among hills or mountains where there is a lot of rain. A dam is built across a river to make a reservoir. The power station is at the bottom of the dam. Here, because the water is very deep, it has a great deal of **pressure**. This pressure pushes the water at high speed through a pipe to the power station. Here, the force of the water turns a huge waterwheel called a **turbine**. The turbine drives another machine called a **generator**, which makes electricity. Then **cables** carry the electricity to houses, farms and factories.

An undershot water wheel in Syria

Cables taking electricity to factories and homes

Dam

Hydroelectric power station

Generator

Turbine

Moving wheels

When you boil water in a teakettle, steam comes out of the spout. If you put a cork in the spout, the steam lifts the lid up and down. A steam engine works somewhat like this. But instead of a lid, the steam pushes a rod called a **piston** up and down or back and forth.

Over 200 years ago James Watt, a Scottish inventor, made a powerful steam engine that turned a wheel.

Years later, people began to attach steam engines to wheels. Soon after, the railroad steam locomotive and the paddle-wheel steamboat were invented.

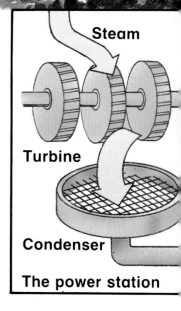

Steam

Turbine

Condenser

The power station

A steam engine made in 1878. It gave power to run a machine but was moved about by horses.

Power stations use steam to make electricity. A **furnace** heats a boiler of water. Jets of steam turn a **turbine** that rotates at great speed to run a **generator,** which makes electricity. The steam then goes to a **condenser** to be cooled back into water.

In some parts of the world, hot water and steam escape from the ground through cracks. Underground water is heated by hot rocks deep down inside the Earth. This natural steam is piped to power stations to make electricity. It is called geothermal power. "Geo" means "earth" and "thermal" means "heat."

Generator

Electricity

Water

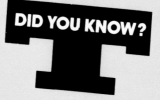

DID YOU KNOW?

Natural steam
Natural steam was first used at Lardarello in Italy in 1904. Today, it is used to heat houses and run Italian trains. Just one little problem — the power station gives off a gas called hydrogen sulfide, which smells like rotten eggs. Phew!

Life was completely changed by the steam engine. Steam engines were used to power ships and trains. They also powered huge machines in factories and on farms.

Too little

Many people in the world do not have enough water to drink or to grow crops. They live in hot, dry lands or deserts that have very little rain.

Plants will not grow without water. They need **moist** soil. The farmers have to take water from the nearest well or river to the fields. This is called **irrigation**. Pictures over 4,000 years old show farmers irrigating their land. Some people use the same **methods** today.

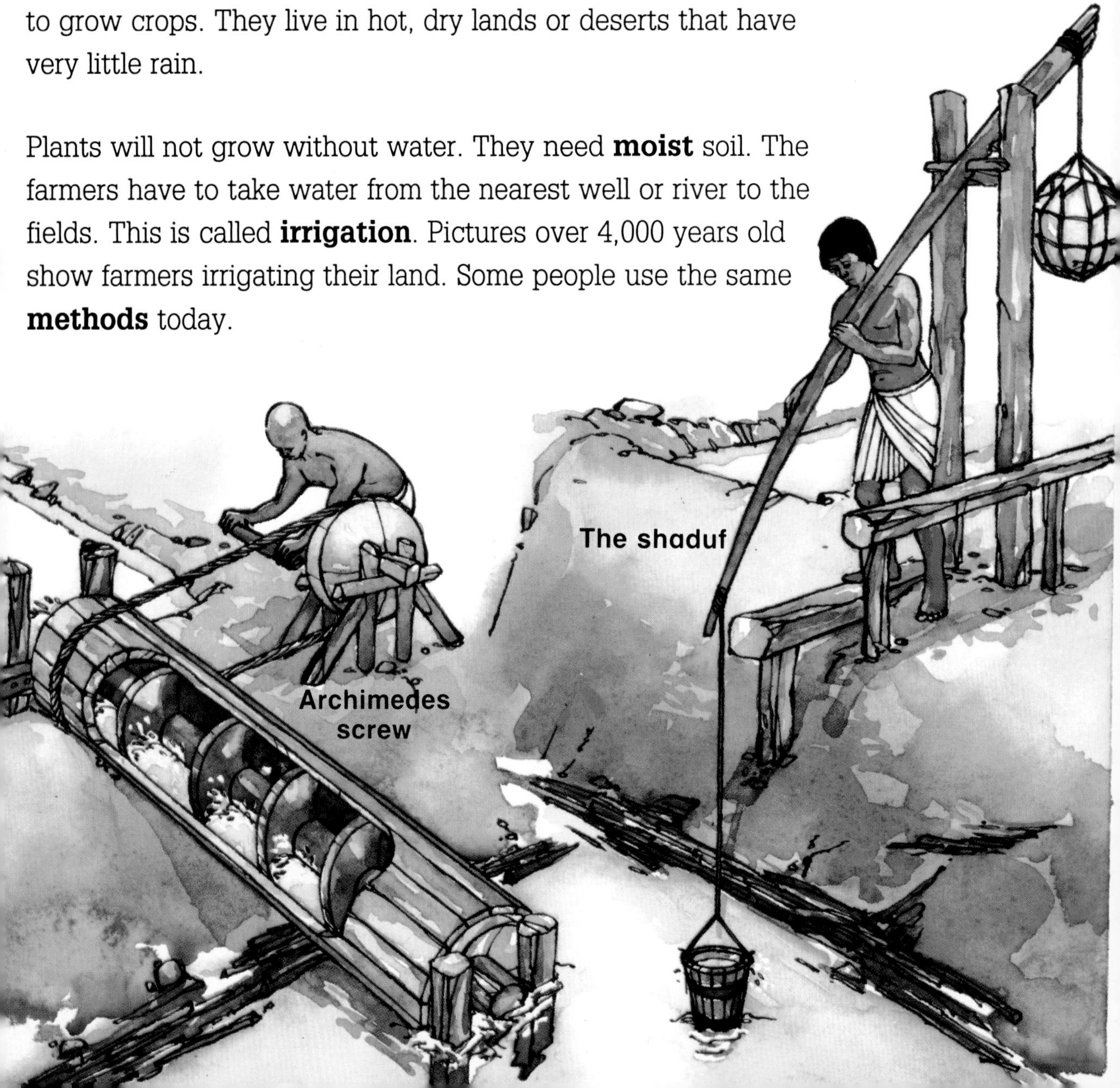

The shaduf

Archimedes screw

Water is carefully stored for the sheep in Australia

Irrigation in Egypt

In some countries, rain only falls at one time of the year, the rainy season. This water must be saved until it is needed in the dry season.

Usually a dam is built across a river to collect the rainwater in a **reservoir**. The water is then used in the fields in different ways. Sometimes a lot of water is released at once to flood the land. Usually, the water is led into canals or **irrigation channels**. Another method is to send the water through pipes into sprinklers, which spray the crops with water.

In other countries, there are good supplies of water under the ground. A deep well is drilled into the ground and the water is drawn up with electric pumps.

Too much

Heavy rain or melting snow can make a river flood. It overflows its banks and covers the surrounding land, called a floodplain. There are towns on some river floodplains, so floods can be very dangerous.

The sea also causes floods along the coast when there is a very high **tide**. In Holland they build dikes, or dams, to prevent this. Some rivers have big gates called **sluice gates**. They stop the sea from entering and causing a flood.

Flood water in India

Flood risk area

Thames barrier

London

UNITED KINGDOM

English Channel

The Thames River in London used to flood during a high tide. A new flood barrier was opened in 1984. It has a series of gates across the river. The gates are raised when a flood tide is expected. Computers receive information about wind and tides and decide whether the gates should be raised. They seal off the river from the sea with a **steel** wall, 65 feet high.

In Holland the land has to be protected from high tides. The land behind the dikes is lower than the level of the sea. It is in constant danger. In 1953 storm tides caused a flood that killed over 1,500 people. The Delta project is a series of dams built to prevent flooding. When a flood tide is expected, sluice gates are lowered against the sea.

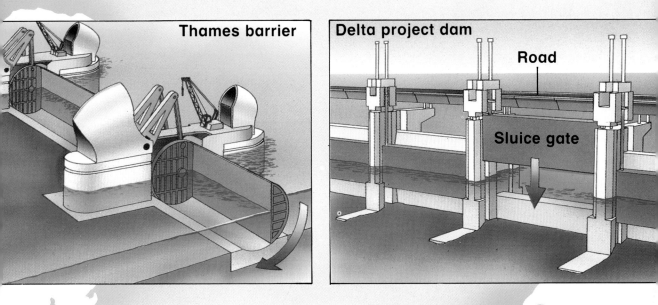

Thames barrier

Delta project dam

Road

Sluice gate

North Sea

Delta project dams

Rotterdam

Flood risk area

The delta of the Rhine River

• Antwerp

HOLLAND

Water for life

BEGIN HERE

Water is essential for life on Earth. It behaves in a very special way. It can be solid when ice, liquid when water and invisible in air. You are going to find out about some of the special things water can do.

First of all, look at these two pages. Read **Look around** and the story about the donkey. On page 30 there are some investigations for you to try.

Finding out about something is called research. You are doing research into how water behaves. Try to make notes about your research while you are doing it. They help you remember later on.

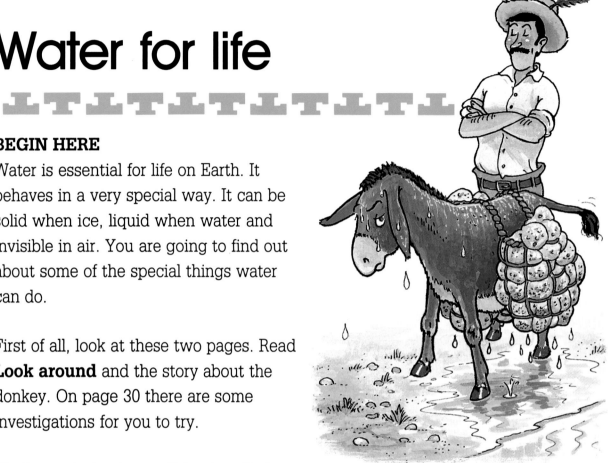

The donkey and the pond

A farmer and his donkey were walking home from market on a hot, sunny day. The donkey groaned. The sacks of salt on his back were heavy. He could hardly walk. Suddenly he tripped and fell into a pond. SPLASH!

The farmer was furious. "My salt! Get up you silly donkey!" The donkey was enjoying the cool water. He stood up

Look around

Some people live in countries where there is a lot of rain, others in countries where there is not very much. Do you think you live in a place with a lot of rain? You could keep a record of how much rain falls. You will need to make a rain gauge, which is a container to collect the rain. You can make it from an old bottle. Place your rain gauge in an open place, not under a tree or near a wall. Make sure it will not blow over. Collect the rain at the same time each day. Measure how much rain there is and record your results on a chart. Do this for a month. Which was the wettest day? Which was the driest week?

Places to visit

Your local waterworks
A working watermill
A local river
A power station
A dam and reservoir
A working steam engine
A village well
A talk with a plumber

Words to know

You will come across some unusual words in your investigations. If you do not know the meaning of a word, you could try the Word List on page 31 of this book, or better still, use a dictionary. Here are some of the words you may need to look up:

soluble   solution
insoluble   properties
absorb

slowly. His load felt much lighter. Of course it did. The salt had dissolved in the water. "Yippee," thought the donkey, trotting along feeling cool and light.

The next day the donkey came staggering along under an enormous load of sponges. He saw the pond ahead. He had an idea! He tripped, on purpose, into the lovely cool water. The farmer smiled. The donkey tried to stand up. His load felt much heavier. He struggled out, looking very cross and puzzled. "Your trick didn't work," laughed the farmer. "Sponges absorb water, which makes them heavier. You silly old donkey."

Evaporation

Get a small jar and a saucer. Fill the jar with cold water and then empty it into the saucer. Fill the jar again. Place the jar and saucer on a windowsill or shelf. Look at them after a few hours. Look at them the next day, and the following day.

What has happened? Can you explain why?

Condensation

Get a tin can. Make sure it is dry both inside and outside. Fill the can with ice cubes and then leave it for 15 minutes.

Look at the outside of the can. What do you see? Feel the outside of the can. What has happened? Can you think why?

Dissolving things

Put about 2 inches of cold water into a beaker. Add one teaspoonful of sugar. What happens?

Now stir the water. What happens?

Try this again using warm water. Does it make a difference?

Try dissolving other things in cold and warm water. Try gravy powder, coffee, soap, curry powder, soap powder, talcum powder. Make a record of each in the chart below.

Ask someone to give you a teaspoon of bicarbonate of soda. What happens to that?

Do not taste any of the solutions.

Things that don't dissolve (insoluble)	Things that dissolve slightly	Things that dissolve (soluble)

TAKE IT FROM HERE

You have found out some of the things that water can do. You could make your own book called *Water for Life*.

Perhaps you can find poems and stories about water. Can you make up a piece of music that sounds like running water. You could try to make a model of a waterwheel that really works.

Things you need

Small jar	Gravy powder
Saucer	Coffee
Tin can	Soap
Water	Curry powder
Ice cubes	Soap powder
Beaker	Talcum powder
Teaspoon	Bicarbonate of
Sugar	soda

aeration tank (page 18) A tank of water or other liquid through which air is pumped.

automatically (page 16) Something that works by itself until the job is finished.

ball valve (page 14) A way of turning off the water when it reaches the right level. A hollow ball floats on the water. It is attached to a kind of faucet called a valve. As the water rises, the ball and a rod rise. At the right level, the faucet shuts off the flow of water.

chlorine (page 14) A gas with a strong smell. It is often used in swimming pools to kill germs.

concrete (page 12) A mixture of sand, gravel and water that flows like mud when it is new but becomes very hard.

digest (page 18) To change food inside a body so that the body can use it.

dissolve (page 10) Disappear into a liquid, like sugar into tea or coffee.

effluent (page 19) Waste liquid flowing out of a factory into a river or the sea.

engineers (page 12) People who are experts in designing and building things, like machines and roads.

evaporates (page 10) Dries up and disappears into the air.

fertilize (page 18) To add things to the soil so that plants grow better.

filter bed (pages 14 and 18) A kind of strainer made of sand and gravel that cleans dirty water.

fresh (pages 6 and 12) Water that is not salty.

furnace (page 22) A kind of oven that gets very, very hot.

inventions (page 16) Machines built by people using new ideas.

irrigation channels (page 25) Narrow gulleys that carry water to plants.

methods (page 24) The ways in which something is done.

millstones (page 20) Two flat, round stones used for grinding grain.

moist (page 24) Damp or slightly wet.

overshot (page 20) A waterwheel that turns when water flows over the top.

piston (page 22) A round plug on a rod that fits inside a tube and is pushed backward and forwards by steam or gas.

pollution (page 19) Spoiling land, air or water with rubbish or chemicals.

pressure (page 21) A steady push.

reservoir (pages 12, 14 and 25) A place for storing large amounts of water.

settling tanks (page 18) Tanks in which liquid can be left to allow particles to sink and settle to the bottom.

sludge (page 18) A thick, sticky mud.

sluice gate (page 26) A sliding gate that controls the flow of water in a canal or river.

steel (page 27) A strong metal made from iron.

tide (pages 11 and 26) The coming in and going out of the sea. This happens twice a day but at different times each day.

undershot (page 20) A waterwheel that turns when water flows underneath.